UNOFFICIAL

Taylor Swift
Christmas

COLORING BOOK

MW00862257

chartwell
books

TIS
THE
SEASON
FOR
CREATIVE
COLORING

Celebrate the most wonderful time of year with the world's favorite superstar!

With over 200 million records sold, 300+ award wins, and multiple record-breaking world tours, Taylor Swift has captured the hearts of millions around the globe, and now she's here to help you celebrate the holiday season.

Growing up a December baby on her parent's Christmas tree farm, there are more than enough reasons for our favorite famed storyteller to get a Christmas-themed makeover. With a voice fit for the season and enough songs to foster the festive spirit and fight those winter blues, a Taylor Swift Christmas is the perfect holiday for the diehard Swifties and newly certified fans alike!

In these pages, you can harness your artistic talent with delightful holiday images sure to please any Swiftie. Whether you're an experienced coloring enthusiast or just starting out, you can create vibrant, finished pieces of art in whatever way you'd like. In addition to every Taylor-inspired image, on the back of each page is an intricate meditative pattern to bring to life with your own unique touch.

If you're looking to destress, unlock your inner creative, or add some Taylor-themed fun to your holiday season, these festive coloring pages will keep you entertained throughout your Christmas era!

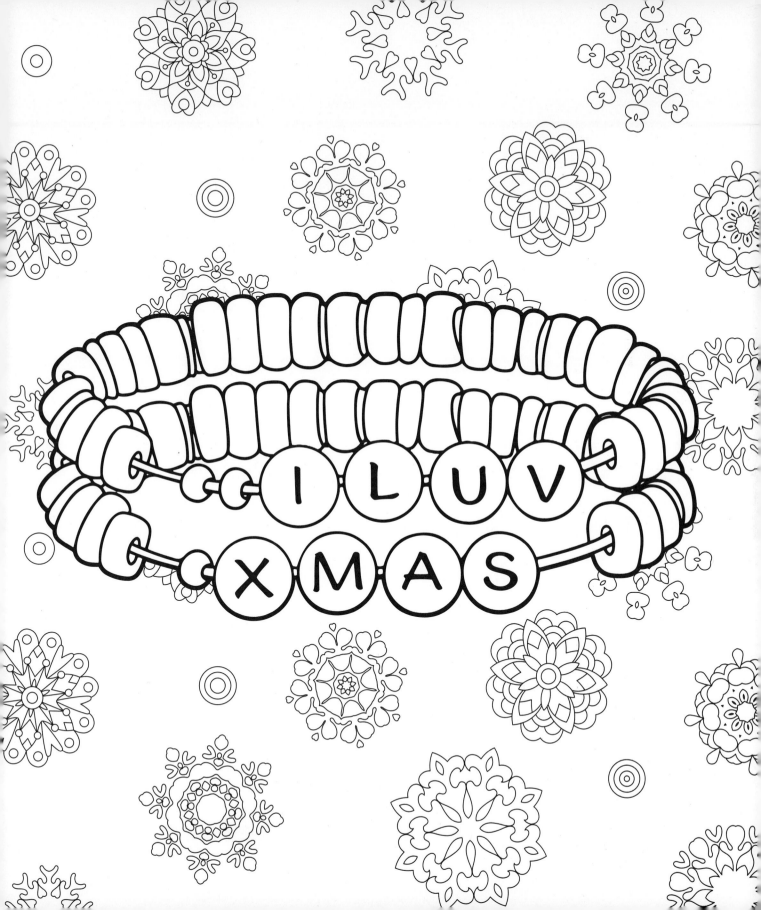

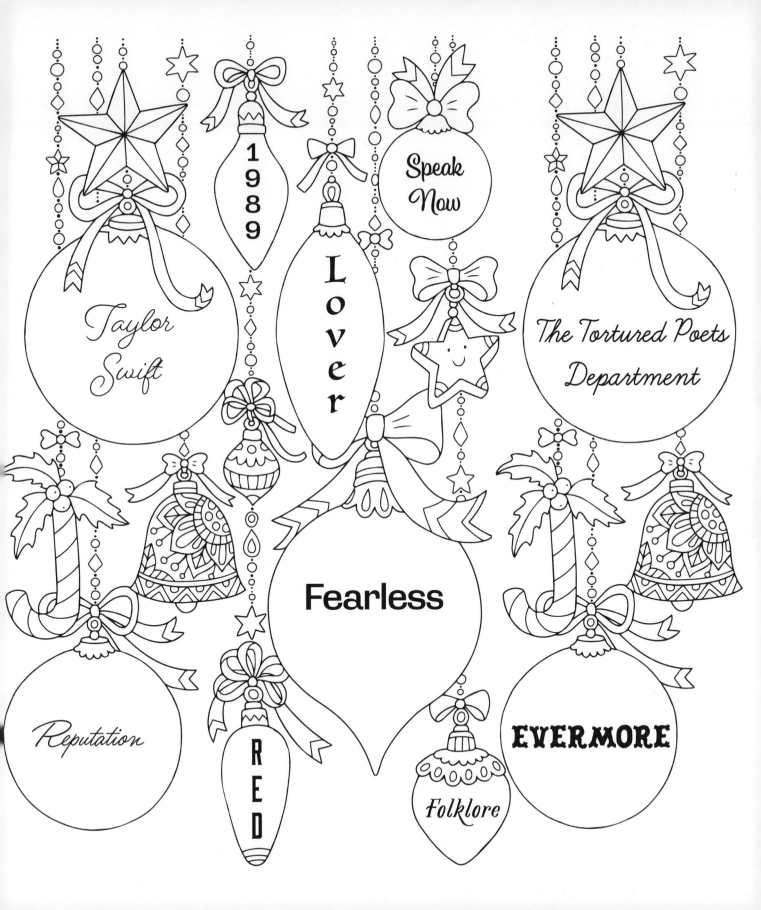

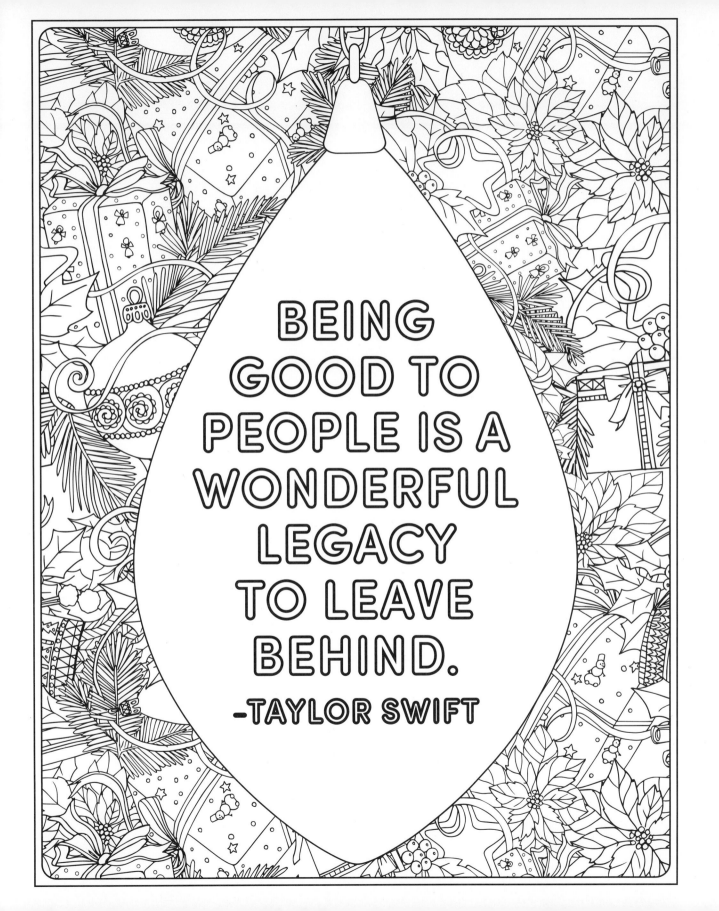

Under the mistletoe

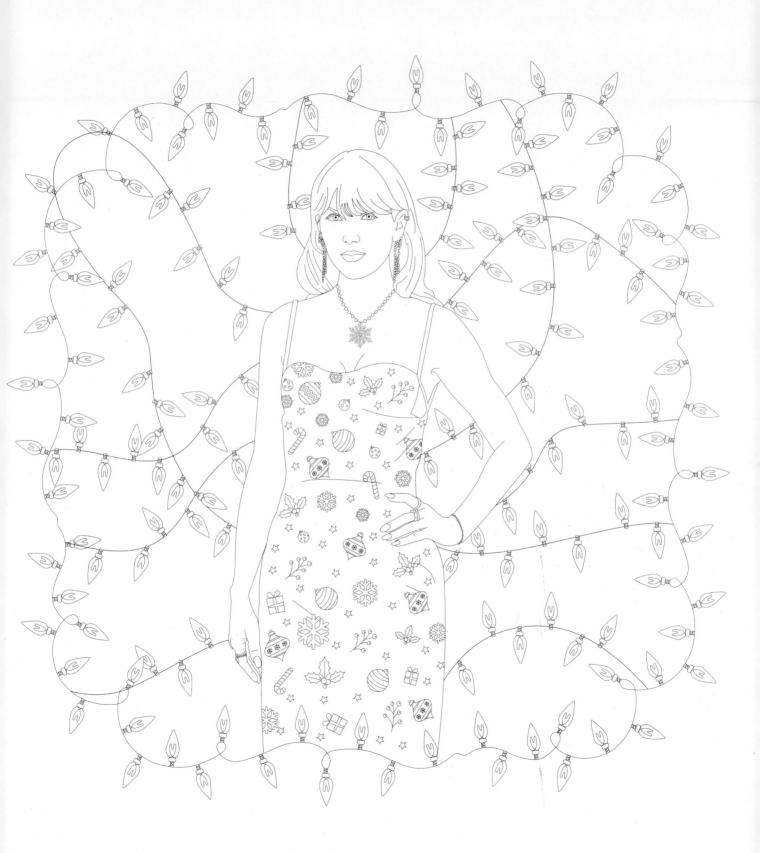

Quarto

© 2024 Quarto Publishing Group USA Inc.

This edition published in 2024 by Chartwell Books,
an imprint of The Quarto Group
142 West 36th Street, 4th Floor
New York, NY 10018 USA
T (212) 779-4972 F (212) 779-6058
www.Quarto.com

All rights reserved. No part of this book may be reproduced in any form without
written permission of the copyright owners. All images in this book have been
reproduced with the knowledge and prior consent of the artists concerned, and no
responsibility is accepted by producer, publisher, or printer for any infringement of
copyright or otherwise, arising from the contents of this publication. Every effort has
been made to ensure that credits accurately comply with information supplied. We
apologize for any inaccuracies that may have occurred and will resolve inaccurate or
missing information in a subsequent reprinting of the book.

10 9 8 7 6 5 4 3 2 1

Chartwell titles are also available at discount for retail, wholesale, promotional,
and bulk purchase. For details, contact the Special Sales Manager by email at
specialsales@quarto.com or by mail at The Quarto Group, Attn: Special Sales
Manager, 100 Cummings Center Suite 265D, Beverly, MA 01915, USA.

ISBN: 978-0-7858-4537-9

Publisher: Wendy Friedman
Senior Publishing Manager: Meredith Mennitt
Designer: Angelika Piwowarczyk
Editor: Caitlyn Ward
Image credits: select illustrations by Jamie Jones; select illustrations by Simon and
Sons; All stock design elements ©Shutterstock

Printed in China